How to improve customer satisfaction in times of spending cuts

HOWARD DOBSON

Copyright © 2018 Howard Dobson

All rights reserved.

ISBN-13:
978-1727146875

ISBN-10:
1727146875

CONTENTS

	Introduction	i
1	What is customer satisfaction?	1
2	Why is customer satisfaction important?	4
3	The difference between actual and perceived levels of service	6
4	Customer relationship	11
5	Good communications	17
6	Strategic communications planning	23
7	Ethics	42
	Final words	43
	Useful websites	45
	References	46

INTRODUCTION

This book is more than an introduction to customer satisfaction - it is an easy-to-use guide to improving customer satisfaction scores. Drawing from original research and extensive reading, it teaches you to make the right moves to improve satisfaction without increasing your budget. How is that possible? Continue reading and you will discover that there is more to customer satisfaction than you thought. You might even find that you can improve your scores while reducing your budget – a double win.

The know-how needed to bring this about is explained through a succession of easy-to-read chapters. First of all I define customer satisfaction, then I outline why improving your scores is important. We then look at the factors that contribute to customer satisfaction before outlining the techniques that can be used to get results that don't impact on your budget.

These techniques could be employed in any sector but are probably most essential in the public sector, where they can improve satisfaction in any field where customer approval is a priority, including highways, waste, community health and countryside services.

1 WHAT IS CUSTOMER SATISFACTION?

There is a lot to customer satisfaction. Keeping customers satisfied is a difficult business. Services can be run efficiently and expertly and yet sometimes customer satisfaction scores can be as low as 40 per cent, 30 per cent or even 20 per cent when the teams involved deserve a much better rating.

There are various definitions of customer satisfaction including: "The number of customers, or percentage of total customers, whose reported experience with a firm, its products, or its services (ratings) exceeds specified satisfaction goals" (Farris, Bendle, Pfeifer, Reibstein, 2010).

This definition is useful for focus but we need to go in deeper if we are going to improve our satisfaction scores.

First of all let's look at customer satisfaction from the customer's point of view. If we get an insight into how customers are thinking we might be able to respond in a way that better meets their needs.

A good starting point is *The Drivers of Satisfaction from Public Service* report (Cabinet Office) from 2004. Although 14 years old its findings are still relevant today. It shows how customer satisfaction breaks down into a number of categories. The most important finding within the report is that service delivery (for example the quality of adult social care) is said to make up only 30 per cent of total customer satisfaction. This means 70 per cent of satisfaction comes from other areas. These are said to include: timeliness (24 per cent), information (18 per cent), staff professionalism (16 per cent) and staff attitude (12 per cent). Diagram 1 illustrates these findings.

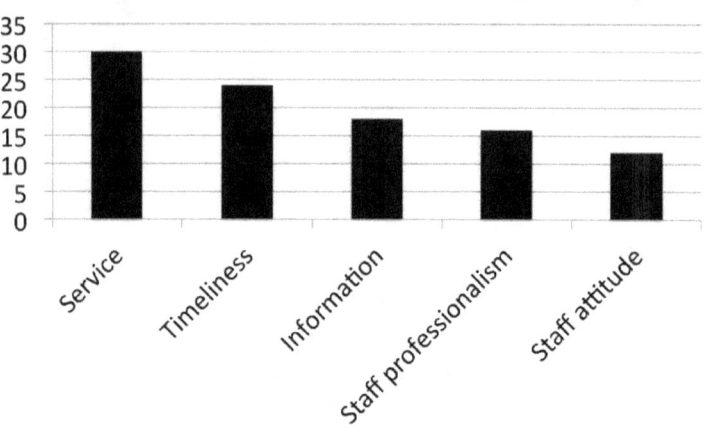

Diagram 1   Cabinet Office/MORI 2004

There is more to satisfaction than providing a service. Customer relationship is also important. You could fill in more potholes or completely resurface the roads to try and improve your scores - but you could potentially move up a couple of percentage points by giving people better and clearer information about your service. You could make sure your staff are always on time and always polite. You could ensure staff are as professional as possible. Helpline staff who know their stuff are as public-facing as electricity workers fixing a broken connection.

This book focuses on improving customer satisfaction during times of public spending cuts - and you can see already that there is scope to improve scores in a cost-efficient way that doesn't involve spending hundreds of thousands of pounds of capital or revenue budget (that you don't have) on new facilities and infrastructure.

However, improving customer relationships is not just about serving our customers well. Looking and sounding professional helps, but we need to be more expert at building customer satisfaction than that. This is where good communications come in, for two main reasons.

Firstly, customers may never come into direct contact with your staff members. Many customers drive along roads and enjoy local parks without interacting with your teams. Improving the politeness of call centre staff and fixing a dangerous pothole in minutes will have no impact on levels of satisfaction for many customers, whereas good communications extolling your strengths will potentially impact more people.

Secondly, customer satisfaction is highly subjective. One person could be very satisfied with a service and the way it's provided while his or her neighbour could be very dissatisfied with the same service. In reality people's opinions are affected by a whole range of things that affect their rating of a service – including their age, background, education, mood, past experience of services in other areas, personality and the quality of communications. Some of these factors are out of our control. Other factors though, such as demonstrating our expertise and our genuine concern for people, are well within our control and if we put together a strategic communications plan we can move up the satisfaction league tables in a way we never thought possible.

We'll get on to making a successful communications plan later on but first a brief look at why improving customer satisfaction is important.

2 WHY IS CUSTOMER SATISFACTION IMPORTANT?

In general the public won't be browsing through lengthy customer satisfaction reports – particularly as some of the more detailed reports, covering several different sectors, cost over £1,000. Some customer satisfaction results are available free online of course but even those figures probably won't be read by the general public. So why does customer satisfaction matter so much?

There are many good reasons for maximising customer satisfaction.

Firstly, good survey scores are a good general measure of success, not just of the service you provide but your ability to communicate your strengths effectively. Hitting KPIs (Key Performance Indicators) is important and customer satisfaction scores may even be reported in quarterly speadsheets compiled for the Cabinet or Board. If your section is doing well, particularly in times of spending cuts, you can feel more secure about your department's future. "Developing relationship management strategies that can be quantified supports one's position within the organisational structure. Conversely, those lacking this capability find themselves vulnerable, particularly during times of cost-cutting and downsizing" (Bruning and Ledingham, 2015: 131).

Councils need to be serving residents well as it is usually a key priority to provide excellent services. Chief Executives will be keen to gather measurable evidence of this excellence as then they are seen to be simultaneously serving their political superiors well. Naturally, the Leader of the Council (or in some councils the Executive Mayor) also wants to be able to show that the majority party is worth voting for. Public approval is one way of persuading people to vote a particular way.

Another good reason for obtaining a good customer satisfaction result is that it can be quoted in applications for central government funding. Often there is a question on application forms seeking proof that a satisfactory customer satisfaction strategy is in place. Results shown to be improving over several years speak for themselves.

3 THE DIFFERENCE BETWEEN ACTUAL AND PERCEIVED SERVICE LEVELS

Understanding customer satisfaction properly means taking on board some key bits of learning – some of which might surprise or even challenge you. Developing your understanding is the difference between succeeding and failing in your bid to improve your satisfaction scores.

The following chapters are based on my own learning, vast reading and academic research, which focused on customer satisfaction with public highways maintained by local highways authorities. The findings can be applied to any public service though and will be explained in easy-to-understand, bite-sized sections.

As we progress through the pages, I'm going to build up a model of customer satisfaction one easy stage at a time.

Actual service levels

The first thing to get to grips with is that customer satisfaction is not strongly linked to the actual level of service you provide. That sounds strange but it's true. When you think about it, it makes perfect sense. How would a member of the public know whether the service they received is good or bad? How do they know if meals on wheels are better in a neighbouring county? Is the treatment and service provided in a local hospital the best in the country or far inferior to a hospital a few miles away? How can they know about highway conditions without surveying all 900 miles of road in a county? The truth is that the public do not know how to make an accurate decision about the quality of a service.

Obviously in the UK organisations like Ofsted and the CQC (Care Quality Commission) make inspections of some services and award an 'excellent' or 'needs improvement' status. This helps the public to rank services more easily if they are aware of the results of such an inspection – but it is still difficult for them to rank two community health service providers with the same overall inspection result.

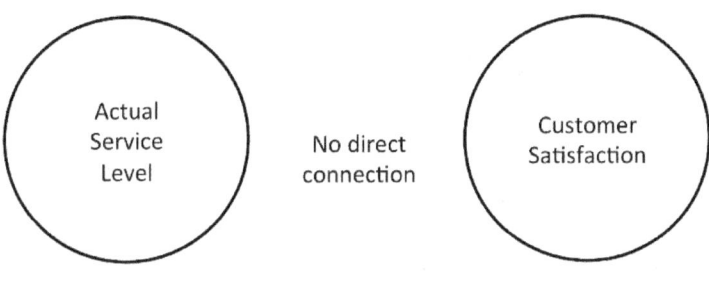

Diagram 2

I observed this lack of connection between service level and satisfaction within my own research. I compared the road conditions in more than 20 local authorities (published by the Department for Transport) to the levels of customer satisfaction with local roads in those areas (published by NHT Networks). Not even a weak relationship existed between actual road conditions and customer satisfaction. What's more, some areas had poor roads yet relatively high levels of customer satisfaction, while others had good roads and relatively low levels of satisfaction. People were happier with poorer roads! This proves that there is more to satisfaction than service levels.

I double-checked this finding by surveying 200 people in three regions regarding their satisfaction with local roads. Again there was no direct statistical connection between actual service levels and customer satisfaction.

The first two pieces of my model of customer satisfaction are easy to put in place as they are two unconnected variables, as shown in Diagram 2.

Perceived service levels

So when customers answer questions on customer satisfaction in a survey, what are they actually reflecting on? As they don't know the actual levels of service they are receiving, they give responses based on their own perceptions of service levels, comparing these perceptions to their expectations of what they should be. As previously mentioned these perceptions could be incredibly biased for a number of reasons. Many customers will obviously give a response based on the service they themselves have received. If they only take certain routes, and they don't think much of the roads taken, they will tick 'dissatisfied' even if the county boasts the best roads in the South.

This kind of bias is extremely common and we can't really blame customers for offering feedback based on their own experiences. They are probably not interested enough in public services to search the internet for hours, rooting through tender documents, full council webcasts and inspection results, to piece together an accurate understanding of service levels.

My research discovered a very weak connection between actual service levels and perceived service levels – see Diagram 3. Customers do base a little of their understanding of services on reality but they also bring their own perceptions into the equation - many of which are not based on personal experience at all. They get confused about what you offer and mix up your services with those of a different organisation. Recycling services differ from county to county, for example, with some district and unitary councils collecting glass bottles, while others don't and expect residents to drive them down to a bottle bank or recycling centre.

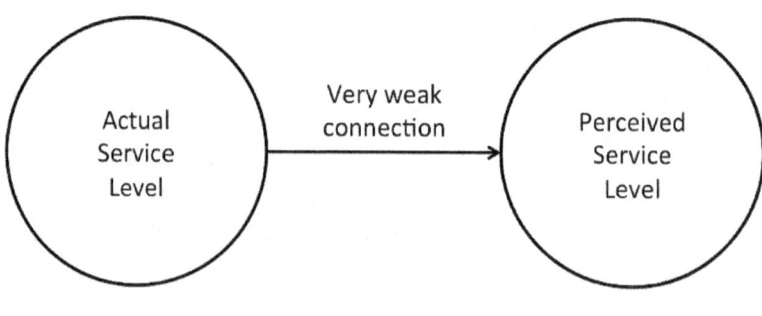

Diagram 3

How to improve customer satisfaction in times of spending cuts

More often than not customers have quite firm beliefs about public services based on political views and sheer prejudice. They may assume that council services are always terrible. They might have seen in the news that funding is being cut left, right and centre and therefore assume that council services, funded largely by grants issued by a government of the 'wrong political persuasion', are pretty poor. That supports their political bias.

A key lesson to learn here is that improving your actual service level won't improve customer perceptions that much.

Realistically though, do your services need to improve? Very often the problem is that the public don't understand how excellent services already are. If they don't currently make the connection between service levels and their own perceptions, how will improving services change things? You may have fallen into the trap of thinking that service improvements are the route to improved customer satisfaction scores but very often that's a dead end. In actual fact your service quality could drop and still be better than customers think it is.

Let's be completely realistic though as you can't radically cut a service to save money and expect that no one will notice. Very large changes to actual service levels – for example cutting 90 per cent of bus services – will, eventually, change people's perceptions of service levels as effectively you are offering a different service.

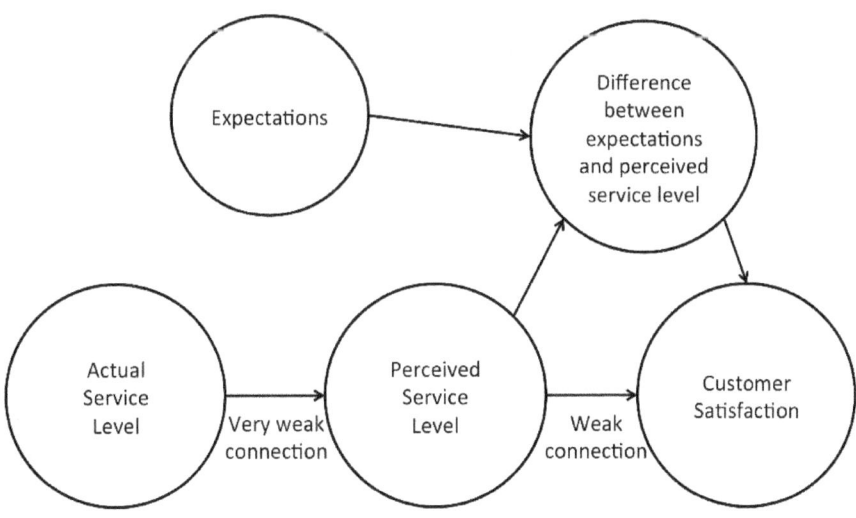

Diagram 4

Within my research I have also discovered that there is quite a weak link between perceived service levels and customer satisfaction. It's less weak than the link between actual and perceived service levels but it's still a weak connection. This is shown in Diagram 4. You can see how the customer satisfaction model is building up as now we have five variables: actual service level, perceived service level, customer expectations, the difference between perceptions and expectations, and customer satisfaction.

Diagram 4 illustrates clearly that if improvements to actual service levels don't influence perceptions of service levels by that much, they are not going to improve customer satisfaction levels by much either, given the weak link between perceptions and satisfaction. It's quite an expensive way to achieve not very much.

Of course organisations could, and do, try to reduce people's expectations of service levels to minimise the difference between perceptions and expectations, but if customers aren't interested in aligning their perceptions with actual service level, they are probably not interested in aligning their expectations with perceptions of service level. At any rate it is ridiculous to lower expectations when service levels are much higher than people realise.

This is where many organisations get stuck as they don't have the knowledge to see the bigger picture. There seems to be no way of improving customer satisfaction and the organisations feel their scores are out of their control.

Thankfully an understanding of customer relationship can make all the difference and put an organisation back in control of its survey results.

4 CUSTOMER RELATIONSHIP

It was an interesting paradox that inspired me to research customer satisfaction. From a set of data I noticed that three councils had strange levels of public satisfaction with local highways compared to the quality of their roads. The council with the worst roads (that is, the highest percentage of total carriageway needing repair) enjoyed the highest level of public satisfaction of the three councils; the council with the best roads suffered the lowest level of satisfaction. These intriguing results are shown in Diagram 5.

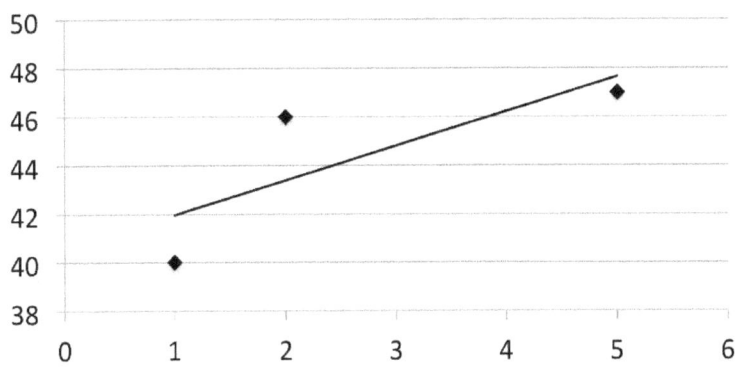

Diagram 5 – the worst roads have the highest level of satisfaction

We've already seen that there is no direct connection between actual service levels and customer satisfaction. So what is it that leads to higher satisfaction with a service where quality levels are not as high?

As a public relations practitioner my instinct was to run a survey asking 200 residents living in three neighbouring areas to answer questions on perceptions of service level, customer satisfaction and customer relationship. I then studied the resulting data to see how these variables related to each other.

The survey results confirmed my suspicions. Residents were more likely to be happy with a service if the relationship between the organisation and the customer was strong. The connection between customer relationship and customer satisfaction was much stronger (around five times stronger) than that between perceptions of service and customer satisfaction described previously.

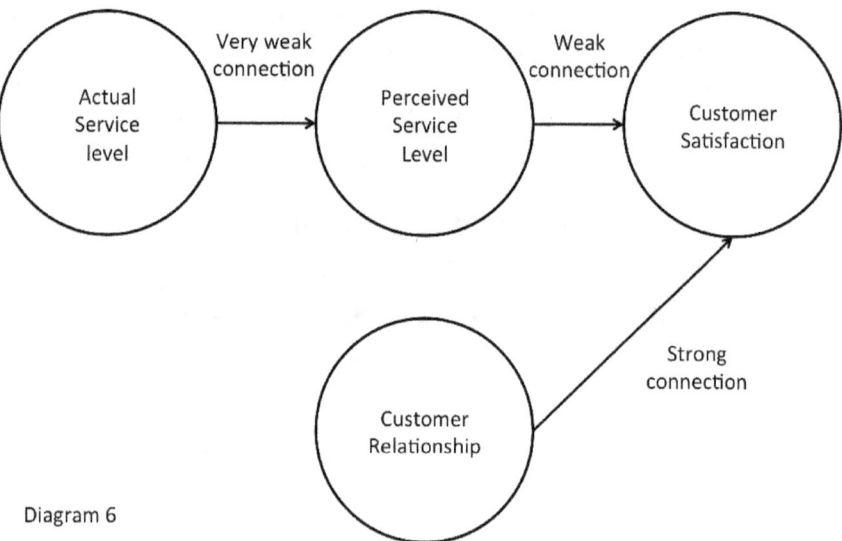

Diagram 6

The diagram above extends the model of customer satisfaction further by including customer relationship and the strong link between relationship and satisfaction.

What we can conclude from this extended model is that customer satisfaction can be increased even if actual service levels and/or perceptions of service levels stay constant or decrease. By strengthening the relationship with customers, whether they be customers of a county council, hospital patients, taxpayers, Job Centre Plus clients or bus passengers, satisfaction scores will improve.

This ties in with what we discovered in the first chapter when we recognised that service levels - more accurately perceptions of service levels - were only part of the story when it comes to understanding customer satisfaction. We saw how perceptions of timeliness, information, staff attitude, staff professionalism and access also drive satisfaction. Now it's time to tie these concepts together under the more descriptive heading of customer relationship.

Understanding customer relationship

Although the term 'customer' might not seem quite right for public services it seems to have become standard. With public services customers tend to be in a different position to customers of, say, a local shop because they often have no (or very little) choice as to who provides their service. There is only one organisation collecting their waste and they tend to be in a particular school's catchment area. This means they are your long-term customers whether they like it or not but hopefully the relationship is sufficiently strong for them to like being your customers.

One advantage of being a public service is that customers tend to know your organisation and what you do, therefore, unlike companies, you don't often have to plan a 'launch' or expensive marketing campaigns to attract new service users and initiate customer relationships.

It is useful to take a closer look at the concept of customer relationships so that we can learn properly how to build stronger customer bonds.

Customer relationships break down into four main areas:

1) First of all, relationships are characterised by the **communicating** we do with our customers. We need to communicate effectively and to listen to customers properly. These days communicating takes place on a multitude of channels and it is important to get it right. It is also crucial for customers to understand that their opinions really count and are an essential part of service provision. Customers need information on the pubic services they use, and generally welcome it.

2) Good communications tends to lead to a high level of **satisfaction** with the relationship between the organisation and customers. This is not the same as customer satisfaction; it is satisfaction with the customer

relationship, not the service. In general a relationship is a happy one if both parties are benefitting from it.

3) When communications and relationship satisfaction are strong, customers tend to **trust** an organisation. They see it as being highly capable of providing a service. They also see it as an honest and accountable organisation. If a road is being resurfaced next Wednesday, customers want to know in advance and they also want the work to actually take place next Wednesday as scheduled. There's more to trust than that though. As well as basing trust on capability and integrity - the 'thinking' side of trust - customers like to feel looked after. If they are happy with an organisation they will trust it more – the 'emotional' side of trust.

4) Finally, relationships can be categorised by **commitment**. We've noted that many public service users are tied to one provider but nevertheless it is still important to build up commitment so that customers have a positive attitude to services and stay in touch with the provider.

A matter of trust

These four elements of a relationship are all important as they tend to link together as a sequence, as shown in Diagram 7. This is a slightly simplified version of how they connect but it is important to recocognise that good communications lead to relationship satisfaction, which leads to trust in the service provider, which leads to commitment to the relationship.

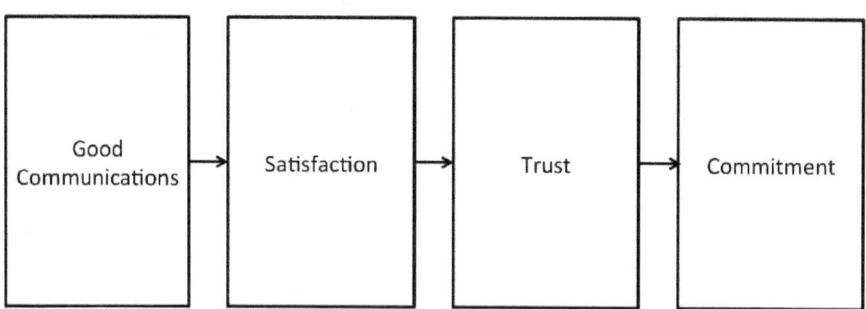

Diagram 7

If any of the four elements of customer relationship should be singled out as the most important it must be trust. This is the element that connects directly, and very strongly, to customer satisfaction. If you don't manage to build up levels of trust you will have difficulty building customer satisfaction via customer relationships.

In my own research, trust was the key to explaining why customers in one area were relatively satisfied with poor roads, while customers in another were relatively less satisfied with the best roads in the region. I discovered that the council with the better satisfaction scores had higher levels of trust. This proves that whatever level of service you are able to provide, customers are keen to be looked after well. If you make a success of relationship cultivation, they may be more satisfied than customers in neighbouring areas.

Interestingly, my research also revealed a connection between trust and perceived levels of service. This implies that with good communications you do stand a chance of slowly improving people's perceptions of service level, which could lead to higher customer satisfaction. Don't depend on this connection though as it is quite a weak link – nowhere near as strong as the link between trust and customer satisfaction.

The full model, containing actual and perceived service levels, customer satisfaction, and the four elements of customer relationship, and including all the relevant connections, features in the diagram below.

Diagram 8

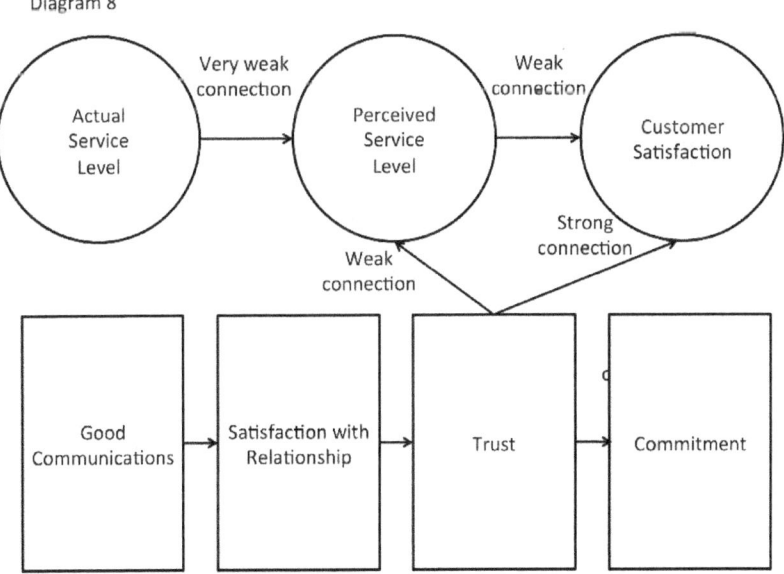

Before moving on to the next chapter, there are a few extra points that are interesting to note.

In my research, good communications and relationship satisfaction accounted for around three-quarters of trust – which means another 25 per cent of trust comes from other sources. It's worth remembering that people will also base their decisions on the communications of others. They may read reviews on websites, letters in the newspapers or comments on social media. If you haven't got a strategy in place to build trust you may find that customer satisfaction is based on unfair comments like "they are always late" or "their staff don't know what they're doing".

Secondly, it should be realised that organisational trust is a concept we encounter every day although we often associate it with related concepts such as branding. Typically we purchase certain products because we know and trust them and the branding helps to give the products an identity so that we can build an ongoing relationship with the brand. Trust in public sector organisations is equally important and you can't take it for granted that your 'brand' is well respected. You need to work at it.

Another related concept is corporate reputation, which is similar to customer relationship, being a product of the various elements that drive trust. Corporate reputation is not quite the same thing as it is possible for a reputation to exist when a relationship does not, based on rumours, untruths and (positive or negative) subjective perceptions. Ideally a good customer relationship should lead to a favourable corporate reputation.

Now we've unpacked customer relationships – and singled out the importance of trust – it's time to look at what steps you can take to make lasting improvements to your customer satisfaction scores.

5 GOOD COMMUNICATIONS

There is an important thing to realise about the **good communications – relationship satisfaction – trust – commitment** sequence unpacked in the last chapter. While you are in complete control of the communications that leave your organisation, the remaining three elements of customer relationship are in the control of your customers. Think of it like tanks of water. You can't fill tanks two, three (trust) and four without pumping water into tank one (look back to Diagram 7). To put it another way, if you want to influence customers, you will have to earn the right to be their trusted influencer.

This means good communications are crucial as without them you won't be able to progress through to higher levels of relationship satisfaction, trust and relationship commitment.

Moving from persuasion to conversation

Many communications offices think of good communications as simply issuing regular bulletins of information, via press releases, tweets or e-newsletters, without any kind of effective communications strategy in place. In the public sector this is usually an attempt to quickly change people's perceptions about a service. Communications leads think that everyone is reading their information and is therefore influenced by it. They think the facts will be absorbed and accepted and assume customers will instantly change their perceptions, opinions and behaviour. Most of the time this isn't the case.

Communications are a lot more effective when they are used to build good relationships via more simplistic messaging, as trusting customers are prepared to believe in your ability to meet their needs, without needing to process and accept or reject all the 'boring' details. "Given total knowledge, there is no need to trust," researcher Daniel McAllister writes. Customers are likely to have only a little knowledge regarding your service, however, and will base a lot of their opinions on how much they trust your organisation.

If you look back to Diagram 8, you will remember that there is only a weak link between trust and perceptions of customer service. Customers are only motivated to read information that directly affects them, not 'chapter and verse'. With some persistence, communications that state the simple facts about a service – such as "we have filled more potholes this year than ever before" - may penetrate through. On the whole any awareness you build will only be temporary and may soon subside and be forgotten about.

Your customers respond to facts such as these in four ways – three of them being a rejection of your message.

1) They may take them on board and allow the power of the truth to change their opinion – possibly moving from very dissatisfied with your service to just dissatisfied, or from neither satisfied or dissatisfied to satisfied.

2) Quite often they will instead think of an additional fact that acts as a counter-argument – such as "that's because you didn't fill in many potholes last year and you need to catch up".

3) Or they may reject your fact out of prejudice, perhaps without even reading your information properly, thinking, "This council is completely useless at everything so I'm not accepting that!"

4) Finally, they could decide that the subject you're writing about is just not important – so they do not bother to even think it through regardless of whether the fact is true or false.

This last point shouldn't be ignored. Many people will decide that gathering information about your organisation is a fairly low priority and may not even see or read your communications. The move to digital media has actually accentuated this as most channels are 'opt in' and so it can be harder to get information in front of people who are more interested in online entertainment.

So we have to be incredibly strategic about how we communicate. This means building strong relationships with customers so that we are not just blasting them with what may seem like random facts. To do this we must communicate key messages strategically by making the most of three core forms of communication: monologue, dialogue and trialogue.

Monologue

Although we often use this word within storytelling, it has other meanings too. In essence it is any type of communication where the information flows one way. Very often organisations only use this type of communication to talk to their customers. While there is nothing specifically wrong with monologue, it can be relied upon too much, leaving customers feeling dissatisfied with their customer relationship, and less likely therefore to trust an organisation. Thinking back to Diagram 7, you can understand that if an organisations relies solely on bursts of monologue, not enough water is being poured into the first tank and therefore tanks two, three (trust) and four are not very full.

It's helpful sometimes to think of personal relationships. If someone talked at you all the time, and never listened, it wouldn't be a very satisfying relationship would it? Customer relationships are the same. There are times when you need to stop talking and start listening.

Monologue can be very useful though within a customer relationship. There are times when you need to explain something using monologue so customers, and other stakeholders like journalists and politicians, have access to the facts. When you are planning to redevelop a town centre, for example, you need to issue documents explaining your thoughts and ideas so that customers can have their say via a consultation or public exhibition. How can you move from a position of relatively low to higher levels of trust unless customers feel you have been completely transparent with them?

Dialogue

This brings us to the hugely important concept of dialogue. Putting a lot of information online about a new development, or uploading a special section on your highways services, isn't of much use unless people are likely to read it, skim through it or at least accept that it's there. There is more chance of information being read and absorbed when effective dialogue is in place.

Dialogue is when communications run two ways – from your

organisation to customers, and from customers to your organisation. Listening to customers isn't just a case of compiling customer feedback that comes in from the helpdesk though. You need to be giving customers a sense that you are responding to what they tell you. Remember that you will have a better chance of improving customer satisfaction if you can create an understanding of your organisation's abilities, integrity and care for its customers. Dialogue is the all-important relationship-building activity that facilitates this understanding.

There are various aspects to dialogue and you should know what they are so that you can base your communications upon them. Here is my top 10 of dialogue essentials that should underpin all of your communicating.

1) The most important thing is to make sure you engage with your customers properly. They must be able to express their ideas, hopes and passions, and empower them with the necessary channels to do so. Interestingly, many public relations scholars say that engagement is the key PR buzzword for the 21st century.

2) You must also regularly demonstrate that your values and priorities are the same as your customers and then listen to their experiences of how your services fail and succeed when compared to these values.

3) In all relationships we should make sure we are present within the relationship to respond maturely and quickly – or at least within an acceptable timescale. No one wants to feel ignored or unloved! You must definitely have key conversations before important decisions are made that affect your customers.

4) Within the ongoing conversation it is important to respect the past, as you build the future. Residents will have warm memories of the old days and acknowledging the contribution of customers, and their families, to the culture of today will help you build trust in your organisation.

5) Empathy is a key concept. Your organisation should encourage contributions to the conversation from everyone, confirming to customers that they are an important part of the decision-making process.

6) Accepting people who are 'different' is a key part of healthy customer relationships. This has been emphasised greatly by the

gradual emergence of today's multi-cultural, multi-faith society. However it has always been an important ingredient of good dialogue as there are so many differences between people – including age, gender, background, education.

7) There needs to be an element of risk within good dialogue. Sometimes you have to say things people don't want to hear – but it's better to say them than to keep them secret.

8) There should be a degree of spontaneity within the conversation as you respond to customers, instead of relying on boring-sounding standard lines.

9) Commitment to the dialogic process is also incredibly important. This means finding shared meaning rather than setting out simply to defeat a customer with an opposing view. There must also be a commitment to interpreting meaning as members of the public do not always say what they mean very clearly. Angry people usually need reassurance not a big argument. Asking people to clarify what they mean is better than assuming they are not making a useful contribution.

10) Last but not least it must be emphasised that genuiness and honesty are essential at all times.

Despite all good intentions it can be difficult to engage customers in dialogue. Many prefer to let others (such as citizen journalists with a blog or community Facebook group, or outspoken residents) do the talking. Realistically, as you can't have a one-to-one conversation with everyone in your area, these unofficial spokespeople play a useful role in bringing opinions out into the open so you can respond and converse in full view of everyone on your channels.

Trialogue

While monologue and dialogue are terms you will have come across, trialogue may not be familiar to you. As the term suggests, there are three people or groups in the conversation. As well as you talking to customers, and customers talking to you, customers are also talking to other customers. This can work two ways.

Firstly, one set of customers can jump in, perhaps on a social media channel such as Twitter, to back up the opinion of another customer who was making negative comments about your service. This clubbing together gives customers an additional way of sticking to their original opinion. It's another version of the second outcome in the *Moving from persuasion to conversation* section – with the opinions of others acting as a counter-argument. You may not be able to instantly able to persuade them all to change their minds but how you respond could still build trust: an understanding of your organisation's ability, integrity and customer care.

Alternatively, you may find that other customers actually support your organisation's opinion, perhaps even jumping in with a persuasive counter-argument before you do. This can be a credible way to change people's minds, with the same power as a five-star online review. If an argument develops between different customers, you may find that your main role is to moderate a sensible discussion with care and compassion, again seizing the opportunity to build all-important trust. Quite often the best outcome is for people to recognise that we are all different and therefore should agree to disagree.

Of course trialogue doesn't just appear on digital channels. Arguments that support or undermine perceptions of your service are, as we have already noted, just as likely to develop in a public meeting or even via a newspaper's letters page.

6 STRATEGIC COMMUNICATIONS PLANNING

Now we've defined customer satisfaction and looked at what influences it, it's time to put a practical plan in place to improve your scores.

To start with it is worth thinking about what sort of increase in customer satisfaction is realistic. It's unlikely that scores will increase by more than a few percentage points in a 12-month period. If you think about the numbers involved, if you had a population of one million adults in a region, you would need, at very least, 10,000 people to move from neither satisfied or dissatisfied to satisfied, for the satisfaction score to go up by one per cent. In a survey sample of 1,000 people, you'd need 10 people to change their opinion in the same way for that one per cent increase. It sounds more achievable putting it that way, but of course with an independently conducted survey you can't just target 10 key people because chances are they won't actually be contacted and asked to participate in the survey.

Targeting your customers

Public relations practitioners always say that you can only talk to the people who are listening. If you have one million people in your catchment area, only a fraction of them will actually be listening to what you say. Even the ones who are listening will probably forget what you've told them quite quickly. I've had big stories run that have been simultaneously on the front page of The Times, on ITV national news and all over the internet, but only those people who were very interested in the story (Church leaders) will have remembered what it was about 24 hours later (the Church publishing tips for dealing with personal debt problems).

It's better to target certain groups of customers and get key messages to them many times so that the information is retained, rather than try and blast everyone with irrelevant information once. That way trust builds and the end result you are aiming for – attitude change – is more likely.

So let's first of all target the people who are in the neither satisfied or dissatisfied bracket, which, let's say, number 400,000 in your region. These are the easiest people to influence so that there are more people in the satisfied or very satisfied brackets. Where are they and how do you communicate with them? Remember, you'd need to change the minds of 10,000 people to improve customer satisfaction by one per cent.

We need to look at the different channels available to us and their potential in helping us build up the three elements of trust: integrity, ability and customer care.

Social media

Many digital channels, such as Twitter, Facebook, Pinterest and Instagram, clump readers into one big group of followers. You are not able to distinguish whether individual followers are satisfied or dissatisfied with your service. This makes targeting your audience more tricky – as segmentation is one of the key aspects of what has become known as digital marketing.

One thing we do know is that social media generally appeals to the under-55s, with Instagram appealing more to those at the younger end, Pinterest appealing more to women, and Facebook being the biggest social media channel overall. You can analyse the breakdown of followers of your own social media channels to see whether your posts need to be tailored to specific demographics.

It's not just about demographics though as how you proceed strategically with a social media account depends on the general composition of your followers. If they are staff members and champions of a specialised service (such as physiotherapy), they are likely to be satisfied with your service anyway. If they are the general public who are following you to get service updates on a miscellany of topics (roads, schools, waste collection), they are likely to be a mixture of satisfied and dissatisfied customers.

In the first case scenario, you are more dependent on your service champions forwarding your posts to their own followers. You could specifically ask them to repost your messages so that they reach a much bigger audience – ideally with a comment to add a sense of trialogue.

In the second scenario, you will be influencing dissatisfied customers directly. Some of your followers on this kind of general account will also be reposting your messages to their followers.

The same posts could, however, be sent in both case scenarios.

Social media channels are useful for building all three aspects of trust, but are more effective at building emotional responses associated with customer care. This is because social media posts have become like little adverts, containing simple text and often pictures or a short video. Individuals and organisations are hoping to catch the attention of followers in the same way a funky advert at a bus stop might stop and make you look. The posts therefore tend to result in an emotional response (such as a like or a repost) rather than a post that makes people think (which will attract more comments or reposts with a comment). Ideally a social media post needs to click through to a website or news article containing something that will build on the other two aspects of trust: ability and integrity.

email alerts

Many organisations, particularly local councils, issue regular email alerts on a whole range of topics - for example, highways services updates. They also issue general round-ups that contain news relating to a specific area. Customers can opt in and opt out of different newsletters by ticking boxes online, depending on their information needs. As with social media you don't need to develop your own distribution system as the emails are distributed by a third party, such as Mailchimp or Gov Delivery.

One of the main differences with email alerts is that lists of subscribers can be segmented – and not just by topic area. This is because you actually have a list of people's email addresses in an online database and you can split them into separate groups depending on your needs. If you run a survey asking people if are satisfied or dissatisfied with a particular service, also capturing their name and email address as part of the survey, you can then group the email alert subscribers according to their responses. You end up with two lists – one for satisfied customers and one for dissatisfied customers. By segmenting the main list into two lists, you can give the different groups different messages, asking one group for their positive third party testimonies, which you can then use (anonymously if need be) to influence your dissatisfied group. You may well find that you are able to target a few thousand dissatisfied customers this way – from your target of 10,000.

Obviously the large online retailers are able to send you highly personalised emails based on your past orders and searches, but these kinds of alert are out of the price range of most public sector organisations.

Don't forget that you need to respect GDPR (General Data Protection Regulation) requirements when collecting people's personal information.

email alerts are useful for building up the integrity and ability elements of trust.

Websites

We've been using websites for 25 years and despite the passage of time they are still the main hub for information about organisations. The difference between websites and social media is that you are generally expecting customers to make the effort to visit your website regularly to get the information they need. Social media and email alerts, on the other hand, push information through to people at a time of your choosing.

Public relations researchers Michael Kent and Maureen Taylor listed four ways for organisations to earn themselves more website visits.

1) Organisations should maximise the usefulness and readability of the information available.
2) The site should be easy to navigate to encourage visitors to stay and read several web pages while visiting.
3) There should be encouragement to return to the site regularly, perhaps via regular updates so that the pages don't look static when people return.
4) There should also be an opportunity for customers to feedback their thoughts and opinions.

Web statistics are a useful way of tracking how well you are doing on these four principles. Google Analytics, when set up properly by your webmaster, will give you statistics on unique visitors, page stickiness (how long people stay on a page), bounce rates (when people read one page and leave the site) and total length of stay.

Ideally, channels should work together to influence customers. Not everyone is going to read the information you push out but you will be influencing more people overall if you send out regular posts to your followers and subscribers so that, realistically, a proportion of them click through to your site.

Websites are also useful for building up the integrity and ability elements of trust.

Newspapers and magazines

Don't write off newspapers and magazines as being old fashioned. As well as their 'hard copies', they probably have their own websites and social media feeds – and may have more visitors and followers than your organisation does. This makes perfect sense as they are a hub of interesting content that has been professionally edited by trained journalists to make it all a good read. Their visitors and followers may never sign up for your own digital content, so you are reaching thousands of additional dissatisfied customers via their channels for free.

For a journalist to run a story you will need to give them something interesting. They work to proper news values, which organisations tend to forget. Your story needs to be of interest to a lot of people, ideally focusing on something close to home, and ideally something unexpected or quirky. There needs to be a good 'storyplot' too. Many media stories involve a 'victim' and a 'villain' and perhaps a 'rescuer'. It's a classic formula. In a regional publication, the victims could be local people suffering from flooding, the villain is of course the bad weather, and the rescuer could be the council moving everyone to safety. You've proven your ability to react and your caring concern in one trust-building story.

Another good storyplot focuses on a particular person's transformation from hopelessness to hope – this character story acting as a case study of what your service can offer people. Or you could focus on the pursuit of excellence, perhaps an award win or a service innovation. Whatever your story, it ideally needs some pace/action, plenty of facts and some interesting comment.

Journalists also tend to be more interested when they get an exclusive first run of the story – even if you send out the same story as a press release later on. Why should a journalist run something that you've already sent out to tens of thousands of people on your own channels?

A good news piece would particularly help build up the elements of trust relating to integrity and ability. You could also 'mythbust' by tackling a misconception about your service to change perceptions, assuming you have an indisputable killer fact that will change people's opinions. If you want your messaging to have a lasting impact you will have to repeat the messaging through a series of regular news pieces otherwise audiences will start to forget what you have been telling them.

Don't forget that some customers are not interested in the topic but can be influenced positively by an attractive photo or a catchy headline.

If the piece is simply an exclusive social media post, news values still apply but something light and quirky often gets the most reposts, possibly building the emotional element of trust, or possibly leading to a very basic feel-good factor, which could persuade the public to have a positive attitude towards your service.

Essential news updates, such as a road closure for roadworks, could also be of interest to journalists as a quick social media piece, a simple variation of a pursuit of excellence story of interest to the people using that route, but it may be harder to get your key messages included in those kinds of post alongside the update. Remember that information on its own isn't that persuasive.

Keep in regular contact with your local journalists so you can share your ideas and pick up some tips on what they might be interested in running.

Don't forget that comments on newspaper articles, blogs and social media feeds owned by others are often where a conversation on your service flares up. You may wish to contribute and thank people for their comments and suggestions.

Advertising

Promotional adverts can take many forms: newspaper and magazine adverts, posters, billboards, hoardings on the side of buildings, leaflets through doors. With adverts you are in control of the message, in that as you are paying for the advert you can say whatever you like without the messaging being edited in some way. You can also be in complete control of the colours, pictures and graphics you use.

People don't tend to look at adverts for very long and you only have a couple of seconds to get across what you want to say. This often favours emotional communicating as it's quicker to get across a feeling than a point of view. This is why adverts tend to be a good way of introducing people to a new product. In the case of public services you may be able to get across a simple fact or point to build up an acceptance of your organisation's abilities and integrity but you need to keep it simple.

Councils and other public service providers have plenty of sites where they can erect their own billboards and hoardings, which will then be seen by thousands of motorists or pedestrians every day. Although digital marketing has sabotaged some of the terminology, the idea of driving traffic to a site is not a new one.

Digital advertising

It's still advertising but the main difference with digital advertising is that on many channels customers can click through to a web page instantly, making it possible to capture someone's attention with an advert before driving them through to a site for some persuasive facts and figures.

There are various options: you can book display adverts of various sizes on Google or Facebook, for example, or you can 'boost' one of your social media posts to a larger audience, choosing how many people you boost to and target demographics. This is relatively inexpensive and with the right messaging you could make an impact on your satisfaction scores, as long as your campaigning is repeated often enough to be effective.

You can also advertise on video and music channels such as You Tube and Spotify if you feel they reach the right audiences.

Another advantage of digital marketing is that you receive statistics saying how many people received the advert, engaged with it in some way and clicked through to the follow-up information. These statistics are useful but they are not a measure of increasing trust in your organisation. You could have fantastic digital marketing statistics yet suffer from decreasing levels of trust simply because the content was not persuasive enough.

Sometimes organisations have award-winning campaigns in terms of reach, inventiveness and the (temporary) building of awareness, but they are still not experts at hitting targets due to their inability to get their messaging right.

Events

When you organise an event or public exhibition it tends to attract the people most interested in the topics being debated, people with strong opinions for and against. It can be a useful way of meeting and listening to the most outspoken members of the community.

Many people won't be able to make the meeting though and will feel left out. Telling them that they've missed their chance later on won't go down well. Others may think that the meeting is just a legal necessity - a token attempt to give people a say. Ideally events should be backed up by other communications channels – live tweeting, live streaming of a videofeed on the internet, live online Q&A sessions.

You can run digital events too. Customers can tune into a Facebook Live session, listening, posing questions and following the debate. If they can't watch live they can comment later once they've watched the recording.

Online meetings and seminars are other possibilities.

Events help you work through customers' strong emotions and opinions. They help build both customer care and perceptions of your organisation's integrity and ability.

As opinions expressed at events are probably shared by others in the community, it makes sense to address concerns on other channels, such as email alerts, leaflets and web pages.

Building effective strategies

Neither satisfied or dissatisfied

Having reviewed the channels available to us, we need to think about how to solve the problem of moving 10,000 of 400,000 people from neither satisfied or dissatisfied to satisfied.

To achieve this target, we must recognise that it is important to build up trust in all three areas. We can't just build up a sense of emotionally trusting an organisation as the other two elements would be missing. Some studies have concluded that the elements focusing on integrity and ability are a bigger contributor to customer satisfaction than emotionally based trust. It would also seem that high levels of trust based on integrity and ability actually increase higher emotionally based trust. That makes perfect sense as when you trust a person or organisation you feel happy to be cared for properly.

So the challenge is building up trust based on your organisation's integrity and ability in a digital world where communicating emotionally is the norm and customers are only interested in basic bits of information about the services they use.

That may seem like a taller order but it is possible to put together an effective strategy that improves your customer satisfaction scores.

To start with we need to think about where the 400,000 people are currently at in terms of their thoughts and emotions. You could run market research to find out but it is fair to assume that they are feeling fairly neutral emotionally about your service and are not really unhappy or angry about it. We've seen that they are not thinking too much about the service as it's not particularly interesting to them – otherwise they would have a better understanding of actual service levels.

In this situation it would be best to start by connecting with these customers emotionally to build up positive associations with the service. Social media is an ideal place to post positive messages that do nothing more than induce a feel-good factor – particularly as many councils have tens of thousands of followers. This could be pictures of roads being gritted to keep everyone safe, beautiful pictures of rights of way on a sunny day, happy faces at a community centre, a funny or quirky video clip with the potential for reposts. These posts are easy to absorb and understand, generating gratitude and trust even when customers are not hugely interested in the topic. Let's call this **Strategy 1**.

Once some of those 400,000 people have developed some more positive associations with your service, you are in a position to tell them some simple facts that build up an understanding of your organisation's integrity and ability. Again this could be on social media, perhaps via an infographic, poll, game, quiz or activity, or it could be via advertising or email alerts. We'll call this **Strategy 2**.

Not all of the original 10,000 you need to influence will necessarily have graduated from Level 1 to Level 2, and you will have to keep both strategies running simultaneously to capture both segments given that you cannot group customers into segments on social media.

Some of your Strategy 2 customers will accept these facts without disputing them and will be ready for more detailed information about the service. To put this information in front of them, you would have to generate a teasing social media post that invites people to click through for more details – perhaps to a website page, news article or pdf document.

Click-throughs will only occur if you give people good reason to find out more. It's got to be a killer story. Let's call this **Strategy 3**.

Not all customers will progress to Strategy 3 and, depending on their current attitude, they might build up enough trust in your organisation from Strategy 1 and Strategy 2 to become satisfied customers without moving to Strategy 3.

Those who stay at the Strategy 2 level may actually dispute your facts and therefore may respond with a questions on social media, creating a useful conversation where you can back up these facts and moderate a healthy discussion. If these facts become accepted they will be ready for Strategy 3 (and later on for Strategy 7 – see the section *More complex strategies*).

The others who stay at Strategy 2 may not have particularly well-developed thoughts about your service and will benefit from the additional reassurance of ongoing Strategy 1 posts. In reality these customers' attitudes may well actually flip between the Strategy 1 and Strategy 2 levels.

Note though that the emotional side of trust will build as a by-product of customers developing an understanding of your organisation's integrity and ability reducing their dependency on Strategy 1.

It is important, as you can see, to run the three strategies simultaneously to gradually move customers from neither satisfied or dissatisfied to satisfied. What you don't want is to just run the equivalent of a Strategy 1 strategy – as this is unlikely to build up all three types of trust, stunting your chances of improving customer satisfaction. According to my research, if your customers held high levels of emotional trust, but low levels of the trust derived from integrity and ability, the overall level of trust would not be high enough for them to be satisfied with your service.

Table 1 summarises the three strategies, linking them with the types of trust they induce and the best channels to use for each strategy.

Strategy	Trust built	Suggested channels
1	Customer care	Social media Adverts Picture story Videos
2	Integrity and ability (simple)	Social media Adverts email alerts
3	Integrity and ability (advanced)	Website Digital adverts News articles

Table 1

More complex strategies

Dissatisfied or very dissatisfied

So far we have looked at how to move 10,000 customers from neither satisfied or dissatisfied to satisfied to improve our scores by one per cent – but what about all those who are either dissatisfied or very dissatisfied? If there are an additional 400,000 people who are dissatisfied or very dissatisfied, they need communicating effectively and sensitively to transform them into neither satisfied or dissatisfied customers.

Instead of being neutrally emotional and indifferent to the service, dissatisfied and very dissatisfied customers may feel very strong negative emotions such as anger. Perhaps they have spent hundreds of pounds on tyres due to unsafe potholes, or maybe a new development will take away valuable greenbelt land. These emotionally charged customers may or may not also have very strong opinions on your service.

If strong emotions dominate the customer's attitude, you will first of all have to deal with those emotions by also communicating emotionally. Understanding and empathy will have more effect than unfeeling arguments. Videos are very good at communicating on an emotional level, particularly where you can see the facial expressions of the person talking on the video. Exhibitions and events also give customers an opportunity to express their emotions. Their anger might turn into guilt (if they feel ashamed at their irrational outburst), or fear or frustration (if they feel your organisation is not to blame after all for their emotions, it's the 'wheels of change') – all of which can encourage customers to do some proper thinking about the issue. Let's call this **Strategy 4**.

Once the emotions have been addressed the customer will be ready to absorb some facts regarding your service via Strategy 2. There may well be customers who require the occasional reassurance of Strategy 1 of course before moving from dissatisfied to neither satisfied or dissatisfied, or even satisfied.

Where opinions held with certainty dominate customer attitudes, you may have found the customers who are incredibly interested in the topic, perhaps as a politician, someone who works in the sector, a citizen journalist (a blogger or someone with a community Facebook group) or community leader. Their opinions may not be right and very often aren't but the customers will be keen to maintain them and will use every communications opportunity to defend them. Emotional social media posts will have no effect and the only way forward is to communicate indisputable facts alongside key messages promoting your organisation's ability and integrity. These customers may make themselves known in response to social media posts, or may write to a newspaper or even start a blog or protest campaign. This means your communications may be aimed to them directly at a public meeting, via a comments section on a blog, via your own social media channels, or on community Facebook pages. Not everyone with a strong opinion will voice their opinion though and you may need to focus on communicating with the most visible people or groups as key influencers. Let's call this **Strategy 5**.

If you succeed in undermining their opinions, these customers may progress to either Strategy 1 or Strategy 2.

Satisfied or very satisfied

Equivalent situations occur when customers have positive attitudes to your service. You need different strategies when communicating with these customers.

When customers feel very positive in an emotional sense about your service but have a relatively undeveloped sense of trust in its integrity and abilities, you need to communicate very strategically to get people thinking more. This means introducing a negative emotion, very carefully, to stimulate their thoughts. If, for example, you included a hard-hitting video of a car skidding off an icy road somewhere, you could include a couple of lines stating that you will be gritting regularly throughout the winter. This sense of fear makes people think and they are then ready to receive basic messaging about your abilities and integrity. They may have to see this image several times though before fully absorbing the message and moving on to the next level. Let's call communicating with these customers **Strategy 6** bearing in mind that they actually move on to Strategy 2.

Some customers of course will already be satisfied or very satisfied with your service. Their perceptions of the service may be close enough to either the actual service level or their service level expectations, resulting in satisfaction. More realistically they already trust your organisation enough to rate your service highly. In this situation it is still important to retain or even improve customers' satisfaction level. You certainly don't want customers to trust your organisation less and it is essential that you keep on demonstrating its abilities and integrity via effective communications. These customers are already on your side and will be able to cope with more complicated facts and figures via websites, customer magazines and newsletters. You could ask for their positive testimonies as proof to dissatisfied customers that your organisation has high capabilities, via trialogue. That doesn't mean these customers are particularly interested in your topic. Types of road surfacing and the types of machine used to cut grass verges aren't of general interest. Some people might be genuinely interested though and it is worth including links to detailed reports and comprehensive web sections so they can click through to them if they want to. Let's call communicating with satisfied and very satisfied customers in this way **Strategy 7**.

Table 2 summarises the more complex strategies associated with all satisfied and dissatisfied customers, linking them with the types of trust they induce and the best channels to use for each strategy.

Strategy	Trust built	Suggested channels
4	Customer care	Exhibitions Events Videos Social media
5	Integrity and ability (simple or advanced)	Meetings Blog comments Letters in newspaper Social media
6	Integrity and ability (simple)	Social media and website or News articles
7	Integrity and ability (advanced)	Website Documents

Table 2

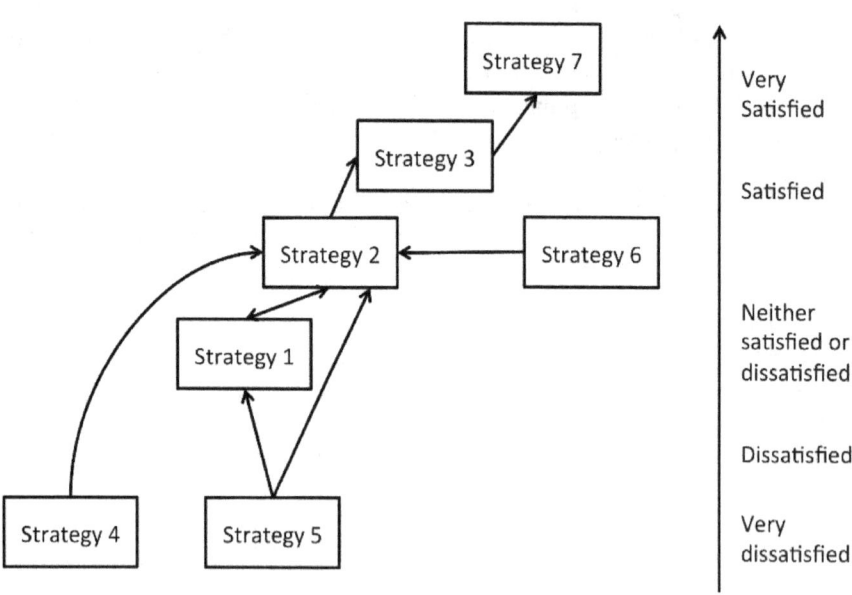

Diagram 9

Diagram 9 compares all seven strategies to show how the right sequence can move your customers from being very dissatisfied to very satisfied with your service.

A key piece of learning here is that it is important to incorporate as many of the seven strategies I've outlined into your communications activity planner as you can. That way you will be moving as many people as possible in the right direction one move at a time, from very dissatisfied to satisfied, satisfied to neither satisfied or dissatisfied, neither satisfied of dissatisfied to satisfied, or from satisfied to very satisfied.

Many of these strategies will be employed simultaneously on some channels, such as Twitter. It is virtually impossible to talk to seven categories of people separately and so you will end up putting several types of post in front of everybody – with customers engaging with the posts that interest them. This has always been the case with public relations though. Within a newspaper some people just read the headline, some the full article, some will look at the photos and others will ignore all of that but will respond to the emotionally charged advert that appears alongside.

Of course you are not able to change the attitudes of all of your customers as they are not all reading your communications. Even those that do see your communications may not see them often enough to move from the neither satisfied or dissatisfied category to the satisfied category. A percentage of them will not be prepared to change their opinions and not all of your angry customers will respond to your efforts to reassure them. Others may only see the emotionally based messaging you post but at least they are retaining some positive attitudes towards your service and are not becoming dissatisfied with it.

How effective your strategies are partly depends on how you construct your messaging.

Messaging

Whichever strategies you employ you are going to need to think about the messaging you include in your communications.

Alongside the information your customers are needing to gather, perhaps on vacancies or road closures or opening times or recycling, you need to plant regular key messages to influence people's understanding of your organisation's integrity, abilities and customer care.

You also need to include key messages that encourage healthy dialogue.

The following messages are recommended within the creative content (words, pictures and videos) of your social media messages, email alerts, websites and adverts.

Trust: ability, integrity

1) We have the skills and capability to do our job well
2) We keep our promises
3) We treat our customers fairly and justly
4) We value your opinions
5) We listen to what you have to say

Trust: customer care

6) We share the same values and priorities
7) You are invited to share your vision and passions with us for this service
8) Everyone is welcome to contribute to this conversation as a partner
9) We care about people like you
10) Thank you for your contributions

Remember that you will need to demonstrate the messages properly – with facts, figures, news stories, case studies, graphics. Obviously the key messages on customer care should be the feelings generated of happiness and gratitude, not necessarily the words themselves.

Also remember that you will need to convey these messages on a variety of levels for the seven strategies – from an infographic or billboard demonstrating promises kept, to an informative web page demonstrating abilities. If some people only drive past a billboard advert or look at your infographics on Twitter, without ever looking at more detailed information, it still may be enough to move them from neither satisfied or dissatisfied to satisfied.

Timetable

As trust in your organisation is essential, you should be communicating on trust regularly.

As a practical guide:

- Communicate all of the simple customer care messages of **Strategy 1** weekly.

- Communicate all of the simple ability and integrity messages of **Strategy 2** weekly.

- Communicate all of the ability and integrity messages at least monthly for the more complicated articles, news reports and case studies of **Strategy 3**.

- Communicate the necessary customer care messages for angry or unhappy customers every two months or so for **Strategy 4** (exhibitions and videos take longer to organise). Bear in mind some angry customers will want to engage via social media regularly.

- Communicating with dissatisfied customers who have a rational argument for **Strategy 5** may also need to take place on a very regular basis on social media, but think of organising meetings to talk through some of these differences of opinion as and when needed.

- Communicating with happy satisfied customers for **Strategy 6** should take place every couple of weeks, particularly as social media tends to build up emotional trust more easily making it necessary to make people think about your organisation's trust and integrity.

- Communicating with satisfied customers for **Strategy 7** should take place every two to four weeks, with new documents appearing on the website and requests for positive testimonials encouraged as trialogue.

You should be using Strategies 1, 2 and 3 as a bare minimum level of activity - but consider using all seven strategies for best results.

Evaluation

A large proportion of public relations strategy documents neglect to include a section on evaluation. This is an oversight as it is important to know that you're your communications are achieving what you set out to achieve. Of course on-purposely avoiding evaluation is a way of avoiding potential failure. Organisations must see beyond this short-sightedness to evaluate projects properly. Only then can they effectively solve the business problem of low customer satisfaction scores.

One obvious evaluation statistic is the customer satisfaction score itself. This is an annual opportunity to see what impact your strategies have had. Ideally, you should set yourself a target score as the main communications objective for your customer satisfaction campaign.

It is also important to measure the trust customers have in your organisation. This KPI will give you an idea of whether trust in your organisation's ability, integrity and customer care is increasing.

Measuring trust means adding a few questions to your annual customer survey - which ideally should come several months before the customer satisfaction survey so that you can set some trust KPIs in advance. You will be able to gauge over time how changing trust scores drive changes in customer satisfaction.

For the trust elements of ability, integrity, dependability (a form of ability) and emotional trust, public relations researchers James Grunig and Linda Hon encourage you to add six questions to your surveys as follows:

1. This organisation treats people like me fairly and justly. **(Integrity)**

2. Whenever this organisation makes an important decision, I know it will be concerned about people like me. **(Emotional trust)**

3. This organisation can be relied on to keep its promises. **(Dependability)**

4. I believe that this organisation takes the opinions of people like me into account when making decisions. **(Dependability)**

5. I feel very confident about this organisation's skills. **(Ability)**

6. This organisation has the ability to accomplish what it says it will do. **(Ability)**

Customers should respond on a scale of 1 (disagree strongly) to 9 (agree strongly). You should find the average of the scores for each question and then find the overall trust score for your organisation by adding the six numbers together and dividing by six.

Be careful not to include the words in brackets such as 'integrity' in your actual surveys. You should of course change 'this organisation' to the name of your organisation.

By comparing your figures year on year you will be able to see whether trust in you organisation is increasing or decreasing. More importantly you will be able to check that the average of the ability-dependability-integrity elements is increasing (not just the emotional element of trust) as this is crucial if customer satisfaction scores are to improve.

Note that there are two questions each for dependability and ability; you should average your results for questions 3 and 4, and questions 5 and 6, to get overall scores for dependability and ability.

You could also add Google Analytics results and social media statistics to your list of KPIs. This will help you see whether your online messaging is working – as improvements in page stickiness and number of social media comments, for example, should be accompanied by increased trust.

In summary, you should set yourself performance targets for your Google Analytics and social media statistics, targets for your trust scores, and targets for your customer satisfaction scores.

Then you need to check that improving digital media statistics lead to a higher trust score and an improved customer satisfaction score.

7 ETHICS

A book on communications wouldn't be complete without a few paragraphs on ethics.

In one line – honesty is crucial if you want to see a genuine long-term improvement in your customer satisfaction scores.

You mustn't try to fake your survey results. We've seen how perceptions of service levels are only weakly linked to actual service levels. My studies have found that more than 85 per cent of people's perceptions are based on external factors such as existing opinions or personal bias. That doesn't mean that you should seek out people who are more likely to give you the results you are looking for. Surveys should always be a representative sample of the population.

It is also important to remain truthful in your communications. If you lied about the quality of your service to try and improve people's perceptions, these lies will sooner or later be uncovered. This has happened publicly with various charities on child protection and safeguarding issues. When the truth finally emerges, perhaps several years later, trust in the organisation is damaged leading to lower levels of approval. Building up trust with the intention of abusing it will certainly backfire.

Accuracy is actually a key principle in the Independent Press Standards Organisation's Editors' Code of Practice (see Useful Websites). Not only is it unethical to state something that is untrue in your own communications and reports, it is equally unethical to encourage the media to propagate untruths. Trained journalists will be well within their rights to accurately report on an organisation's wrongdoings though.

FINAL THOUGHTS

I've aimed to make this book simple to understand, retaining the key bits of learning that are essential for strategic communications planning. As a brief summary, the main points to take on board are:

- Your service is probably better than your customers realise

- Attempts to improve perceptions of your current service level may not be that successful

- Improving your service may not impact satisfaction that much

- Building up trust with customers can be a far more effective way of building customer satisfaction

- You must build up a sense of your organisation's abilities and integrity not just a sense of the customer care element of trust

- You need a strategic communications plan with key messages that goes beyond communicating information updates

- Big numbers from your website and social media analytics are not a guarantee of success

- It is possible to improve scores when your budget has been cut

- You should always be ethical and honest

In the true spirit of customer satisfaction, I am happy to answer any questions you have. To get in touch, send an email to howard@howarddobson.co.uk.

If you think your team would benefit from a training session on the key concepts and techniques I have worked through in this book (at beginner or advanced level), please send me an email to the same address.

USEFUL WEBSITES

Chartered Institute of Public Relations – ethics
https://www.cipr.co.uk/ethics

Google Analytics
https://marketingplatform.google.com/about/analytics

Guide to GDPR
https://ico.org.uk/for-organisations/guide-to-the-general-data-protection-regulation-gdpr/

Independent Press Standards Organisation's Editors' Code of Practice
https://www.ipso.co.uk/editors-code-of-practice

Revelator Photography
www.revelatorphotography.co.uk

REFERENCES

Bortree, D.S. (2015) 'Motivations of publics: the power of antecedents in the volunteer-non-profit organisation relationship'. In Ki, E.J., Kim, J-N., and Ledingham, J. (eds.) *Public relations as relationship management*. New York, NY: Routledge, pp. 144-158.

Bruning, S.D., and Ledingham, J.A. (2015) 'Examining the influence of organisation-public relationships and organisational identification with a psychological group on institutional affiliation, behavioural intent, and evaluations of satisfaction.' In Ki, E.J., Kim, J-N., and Ledingham, J. (eds.) *Public relations as relationship management*. New York, NY: Routledge, pp. 130-143.

Cabinet Office (2004) *The drivers of satisfaction from public service* http://www.customerserviceexcellence.uk.com/UserFiles/File/Key.pdf

Cheonsoo, K., and Sung-Un, Y. (2017) 'Like, comment, and share on Facebook: how each behaviour differs from the other.' *Public Relations Review*, 43(2) pp. 441-449.

Clarkson, J.J., Tormala, Z.L., and Rucker, D.D. (2011) 'Cognitive and affective matching effects in persuasion: an amplification perspective.' *Personality and Social Psychology Bulletin*, 37(11) pp. 1415-1427.

Farris, P.W., Bendle;, N.T., Pfeifer, P.E., and Reibstein D.J. (2010). *Marketing metrics: the definitive guide to measuring marketing performance*. Upper Saddle River, New Jersey: Pearson Education.

Festinger, L. (1957) *A theory of cognitive dissonance*. Stanford, CA: Stanford University Press.

Fishbein, M., and Ajzen, I. (2010) *Predicting and changing behavior: the Reasoned Action Approach*. New York: Taylor and Francis.

Hon, C.L. and Grunig, J.E. (1999) *Guidelines for measuring relationships in public relations*. Gainesviille, FL: The Institute of Public Relations.

Kent, M.L., and Taylor, M. (1998). 'Building dialogic relationships through the world wide web.' *Public Relations Review*, 24(3) pp. 321-334.

Kent, M.L., and Taylor, M. (2002) 'Towards a dialogic theory of public relations.' *Public Relations Review*, 28(1) pp. 21-37.

McAllister, D.J. (1995) 'Affect and cognition-based trust as foundations for interpersonal cooperation in organisations.' *Academy of Management Journal*, 38 pp 24–59.

Petty, R.E, and Briñol, P. (2015) 'Emotion and persuasion: cognitive and meta-cognitive processes impact attitudes.' *Cognition and Emotion*, 29(1) pp. 1-26.

Smith, C.A. (1985) 'Patterns of cognitive appraisal in emotion.' *Journal of Personality and Social Psychology*, May 1985 pp.813-838.

Theunissen, P., and Wan Noordin, W. (2012). 'Revisiting the concept of dialogue in public relations.' *Public Relations Review*, 38(1), pp. 5-13.

Tobias, R.B. (1993). *Twenty master plots (and how to build them)*. Cincinnati, OH: Writer's Digest Books.

ABOUT THE AUTHOR

Howard Dobson BSc MSc DipCIPR MCIPR has worked in public relations and journalism for 25 years, developing communications strategies for local councils, NHS trusts and the Church of England. He was awarded distinctions for his CIPR diploma project and for his masters degree dissertation, both of which developed knowledge of customer relationship management. He is taking a PhD research degree at Manchester Metropolitan University.

www.ingramcontent.com/pod-product-compliance
Lightning Source LLC
Chambersburg PA
CBHW070958240526
45469CB00017B/2463